NATIONAL
GEOGRAPHIC
KiDS

Funny FiLL-IN

MY SAFARI ADVENTURE

NATIONAL GEOGRAPHIC
WASHINGTON, D.C.

How to Play Funny Fill-In!

Love to create amazing stories? Good, because this one stars YOU. Get ready to laugh with all your friends—you can play with as many people as you want! Make sure to keep this book on your shelf. You'll want to read it again and again!

Are You Ready to Laugh?

- One person picks a story—you can start at the beginning, the middle, or the end of the book.

- Ask a friend to call out a word that the space asks for—noun, verb, or something else—and write it in the blank space. If there's more than one player, ask the next person to say a word. Extra points for creativity!

- When all the spaces are filled in, you have your very own Funny Fill-In. Read it out loud for a laugh.

- Want to play by yourself? Just fold over the page and use the cardboard insert at the back as a writing pad. Fill in the blank parts of speech list, and copy your answers into the story.

 Make sure you check out the amazing **Fun Facts** that appear on every page!

Parts of Speech

To play the game, you'll need to know how to form sentences. This list with examples of the parts of speech and other terms will help you get started:

Noun: The name of a person, place, thing, or idea
Examples: tree, mouth, creature
*The **ocean** is full of colorful **fish**.*

Adjective: A word that describes a noun or pronoun
Examples: green, lazy, friendly
*My **silly** dog won't stop laughing!*

Verb: An action word. In the present tense, a verb often ends in –s or –ing. If the space asks for past tense, changing the vowel or adding a –d or –ed to the end usually will set the sentence in the past.
Examples: swim, hide, plays, running (present tense); biked, rode, jumped (past tense)
*The giraffe **skips** across the savanna.*
*The flower **opened** after the rain.*

Adverb: A word that describes a verb and usually ends in –ly
Examples: quickly, lazily, soundlessly
*Kelley **greedily** ate all the carrots.*

Plural: More than one
Examples: mice, telephones, wrenches
*Why are all the **doors** closing?*

Silly Word or Exclamation: A funny sound, a made-up word, a word you think is totally weird, or a noise someone or something might make
Examples: Ouch! No way! Foozleduzzle! Yikes!
*"**Darn!**" shouted Jim. "These cupcakes are sour!"*

Specific Words: There are many more ways to make your story hilarious. When asked for something like a number, animal, or body part, write in something you think is especially funny.

your name

noun

time

noun

noun, plural

silly word

adjective

liquid

noun, plural

noun

noun, plural

noun, plural

adjective

verb

adjective

adjective

noun

noun

Fun Fact! THE **FIRST EVER** CEREAL BOX PRIZE WAS A **FUNNY BOOK** ABOUT JUNGLE ANIMALS.

WACK-O's

MILK MILK

4

Cereal Sweepstakes

"_____ ! Wake up! It's time to get ready for school!" my mom called up the stairs. I wiped
     your name

the _____ away from my eyes. How was it _____ already? I hopped out of _____ ,
        noun   time   noun

threw on my _____ , and ran downstairs. I sat down at the table and reached for the
              noun, plural

_____ -O's, my _____ cereal. I poured it into a bowl and topped it off with
   silly word   adjective

_____ . Mmmmm. Breakfast of _____ ! As I ate, I scanned the back of the box to
    liquid   noun, plural

see if there was a(n) _____ inside. Instead I found this message: "Hey, _____ and
                          noun   noun, plural

_____ ! How'd you like to win a(n) _____ African safari? Just _____ out
  noun, plural   adjective   verb

the slip below and mail it to the address on the box. You could be our _____ winner!" I've never
                                                                          adjective

won a(n) _____ contest before, but I figured it couldn't hurt to try. I filled out the slip, dropped
           adjective

it in the _____ , and caught the _____ to school.
             noun   noun

noun, plural

   noun, plural

noun

   verb

adjective

   color

verb ending in –ing

   animal

verb

   verb ending in –ed

country

   adjective

color

   animal

body part

   exclamation

noun

   verb

Fun Fact! KIDS AS YOUNG AS SEVEN HAVE PILOTED AIRPLANES.

Airplane Escapade

"Buckle your _____ (noun, plural) and turn off your _____ (noun, plural) in preparation for takeoff," the flight attendant announced. I had forgotten all about the contest, but just yesterday a(n) _____ (noun) arrived telling me to _____ (verb) my bags. I can't believe I'm on a plane to Africa! Mom and Dad were _____ (adjective), too. Mom was dressed head to toe in _____ (color) safari gear. Next to her, Dad was _____ (verb ending in –ing) into a box of crackers and picking out all the _____ (animal) -shaped ones. If you can't beat 'em, _____ (verb) 'em, I figured. So I _____ (verb ending in –ed) up and down the aisle pretending I was deep in the jungles of _____ (country) finding _____ (adjective) species of animals. In front of me I imagined a(n) _____ (color) _____ (animal). It was just what I needed for my collection! Lost in my own fantasy, I pounced—and accidentally landed on a man's _____ (body part)! " _____ (exclamation) !" he said. "Sorry!" I replied. I headed back to my _____ (noun). Maybe I should try to _____ (verb) for a while.

- country in Africa
  - exclamation
- noun
  - adjective
- clothing item, plural
  - musical instrument, plural
- verb ending in –ing
  - verb ending in –ing
- your last name
  - color
- type of car
  - adjective ending in –er
- noun, plural
  - noun, plural
- noun
  - adjective
- verb
  - body part
- number

Fun Fact! DON'T **EAT** WHILE **WALKING** IN NIGERIA, AFRICA. IT'S THOUGHT TO BE **RUDE!**

Arrival in Africa

The plane touched down on the runway. "Ladies and gentlemen, welcome to _____ !" the voice
                                                                          country in Africa
over the intercom said. " _____ !" I shouted. "I can't believe we're here!" I grabbed my _____
                              exclamation   noun
and headed for the exit. As I walked out, I saw people dressed in _____ _____ ,
                                                                         adjective   clothing item, plural
playing _____ , and dancing to the beat. Crowds were _____ and
         musical instrument, plural   verb ending in –ing
_____ . It looked like so much fun! I pushed through the group and spotted a man holding a sign that
verb ending in –ing
said: " _____ ." "Looks like our ride is here!" Dad said. We followed the driver to a giant _____
         your last name   color
_____ . When I climbed in, I saw that the inside was even _____ than the outside!
     type of car   adjective ending in –er
It had two _____ , six _____ , and even a(n) _____ ! We began the drive to camp.
            noun, plural   noun, plural   noun
The roads were so _____ and bumpy, I thought I might _____ , so Dad made me stick my
                   adjective   verb
_____ out the window. After about _____ hour(s), we finally arrived at our destination.
   body part   number

- silly word
  - adjective
- something big, plural
  - large number
- noun, plural
  - adjective
- room in a house
  - large number
- noun, plural
  - large number
- something expensive, plural
  - favorite drink
- food
  - number
- noun
  - favorite movie
- somewhere awesome
  - body part
- food

AT A HOTEL IN KENYA, AFRICA, GIRAFFES SOMETIMES STICK THEIR HEADS INTO GUESTS' WINDOWS!

Roughing It

As we pulled into camp I saw a huge sign that said: "YOU ARE NOW ENTERING _____ NATIONAL
silly word

PARK." The driver drove down a road to a group of _____ tents the size of _____ .
adjective   *something big, plural*

He let us out at the biggest one. It was like nothing I've ever seen before! There were _____ rooms
large number

and it even had free _____ ! I grabbed my bag and ran inside. The huge doorway gave way to a(n)
noun, plural

_____ _____ . This place had everything! There were _____ _____ and
adjective   *room in a house*   *large number*   *noun, plural*

_____ _____ , water fountains that dispensed _____ , and a 24-hour
large number   *something expensive, plural*   *favorite drink*

chef who could make me _____ anytime I wanted! In my room there was a(n) _____ -inch flat
food   *number*

screen _____ that was already playing my favorite movie: _____ . This must be what
noun   *favorite movie*

_____ is like, I thought. Just then, my _____ started to rumble. It must be dinner-
somewhere awesome   *body part*

time! We went outside and ate traditional African _____ next to a campfire. What an amazing place!
food

past-tense verb

clothing item

body part, plural

greeting

body part, plural

body part, plural

body part, plural

body part

animal

adjective

animal

animal

animal, plural

adjective

noun

adjective

verb ending in –ing

Fun Fact! A HUGE COLONY OF AFRICAN PENGUINS LIVES AT THE TIP OF SOUTH AFRICA.

Safari Time!

"Rise and shine!" I heard Mom say as I awoke the next morning. It was time for the safari! I _____

_____
past-tense verb

out of bed, threw on a clean _____ , and brushed my _____ . As I ran outside to join the
clothing item   body part, plural

group, I saw a great big safari vehicle waiting for us. "Jambo!" our guide said. "That means '_____!'
greeting

Please keep your _____ , _____ , and _____ inside the
body part, plural   body part, plural   body part, plural

vehicle at all times. You wouldn't want to lose a(n) _____ to a(n) _____ !"
body part   animal

The ride was loud and bumpy as we drove over _____ roads deep into the savanna. Almost
adjective

immediately I spotted a(n) _____ , a(n) _____ , and seven _____ . This
animal   animal   animal, plural

was _____ ! Suddenly the vehicle drove over a huge _____ . Our guide told us to hang
adjective   noun

on, it could get a little _____ . Boy was she right! As I reached for the handle, the vehicle hit
adjective

another rock and I went _____ out the back!
verb ending in –ing

13

verb ending in –ed

body part

adjective

color

type of hat

greeting

nationality

exclamation

adjective

size

number

body part, plural

nickname

noun

body part

animal

Fun Fact! MORE THAN **2,000** DIFFERENT LANGUAGES ARE SPOKEN IN **AFRICA.**

When You Meet a Meerkat ...

I must have _____ my _____ , because when I came to, I couldn't
                verb ending in -ed   body part

believe my eyes. There, standing over me, was a(n) _____ _____ face wearing a(n)
                                                        adjective   color

_____ . I blinked a couple of times, but it was still there. " _____ ." I heard a
    type of hat   greeting

tiny voice say in a(n) _____ accent. It was a meerkat! And not just any meerkat, a talking
                            nationality

meerkat! He told me that he saw me bounce out of the vehicle, but he must have been the only one, because

my ride was gone! " _____ !" I said. Now what was I going to do? I was alone in the middle of
                          exclamation

the _____ _____ savanna, where temperatures can reach _____ degree(s)!
        adjective   size   number

The meerkat started to help me to my _____ . "Look, _____ , it seems like
                                          body part, plural   nickname

you've taken quite a(n) _____ on the _____ . How about you come over to my house
                            noun   body part

for breakfast?" I hesitated, but agreed. What else was I going to do? Sit out here as _____ bait?
                                                                                          animal

- noun, plural
- noun
- same noun
- large number
- name of animal group
- silly name
- silly name
- silly name
- silly name
- silly name
- large number
- adjective
- clothing item, plural
- insect, plural
- insect, plural
- something gross, plural
- reptile, plural
- exclamation
- adjective

 MEERKATS HAVE BLACK CIRCLES AROUND THEIR EYES THAT LOOK—AND ACT— LIKE SUNGLASSES.

Meerkat Mansion

I followed the meerkat into the _____ . "Here we are!" he announced. "_____ sweet
                                    noun, plural   _noun_

_____ !" I looked around, but saw nothing. Suddenly, I saw something moving in the dirt.
same noun

_____ meerkats were popping out of a hole in the ground, one by one! "Meet my _____ !"
large number   _name of animal group_

my new friend said. "This is _____ , _____ , _____ , _____ , and
                                silly name   _silly name_   _silly name_   _silly name_

_____ ... there are _____ others inside. Come on!" I told him I didn't think I would fit. He
silly name   _large number_

looked at the tiny opening and then looked back at me. "Right-o, you probably are a little too _____ .
                                                                                                    adjective

That's okay, I'll send breakfast up!" Soon enough, twelve meerkats wearing little _____ lined
                                                                                        clothing item, plural

up in front of me. Each one held a tiny tray. One at a time they lifted the tops to reveal _____ ,
                                                                                                insect, plural

_____ , _____ , and _____ . "_____ ! No thanks," I said. "I'm not
insect, plural   _something gross, plural_   _reptile, plural_   _exclamation_

very hungry." Just then I heard a(n) _____ voice behind me. "You might not be hungry, but I'm starved."
                                        adjective

17

adverb ending in –ly

adjective

past-tense verb

liquid

adjective

adjective

verb

noun

adjective

adjective

adjective

body part

animal noise ending in –ed

body part, plural

adjective

noun

adjective

body part

Fun Fact! ONE ANCIENT EGYPTIAN TEACHER WARNED THAT VANDALS WHO HARM HIS TOMB WILL BE EATEN BY LIONS!

Scaredy-Cat

_____ I turned around and saw a(n) _____ lioness. I was so scared I
(adverb ending in –ly)   (adjective)

almost _____. Globs of _____ dripped from her _____ teeth. Her
(past-tense verb)   (liquid)   (adjective)

_____ eyes narrowed in on me. She looked as if she was ready to _____! I closed
(adjective)   (verb)

my eyes. I thought I was a(n) _____ for sure! But then, instead of feeling _____ claws,
(noun)   (adjective)

there was something _____ and _____ in my lap. I opened my eyes to see that the
(adjective)   (adjective)

lioness had her head on my _____. She licked her paws, _____ like a
(body part)   (animal noise ending in –ed)

kitten, and asked me to scratch behind her _____. "I don't eat humans, you see. Too
(body part, plural)

_____," she said. "I was hoping you would share your _____ with me!" I breathed a
(adjective)   (noun)

sigh of relief. I told her I was sorry, but I was upset about having lost my _____ group. With that,
(adjective)

she stood up and told me to climb onto her _____. She was going to help me look!
(body part)

19

- number
  - noun
- noun
  - adjective
- adjective
  - color
- adjective
  - animal
- animal
  - year you were born
- animal
  - noun
- noun
  - animal, plural
- noun, plural
  - animal
- noun, plural
  - exclamation
- verb

Fun Fact! AFRICAN ELEPHANTS' **EARS** ARE **SHAPED** LIKE THE CONTINENT OF **AFRICA.**

WILD STYLE TOURS

Animal Tourists

For _____ minute(s), I rode on the back of the lioness, clutching her _____ . No sign of the
       number   noun

_____ anywhere! But suddenly, in the distance, I saw a(n) _____ cloud of dust. Could that be
  noun   adjective

them? I wondered. As it approached, I saw the outline of a(n) _____ _____ elephant, and heard
                                                                  adjective   color

a distinct tour guide voice. "To your left you'll see a(n) _____ _____ , and to the right please
                                                              adjective   animal

notice a(n) _____ ." I saw that the elephant was carrying several smaller animals on its back and was
              animal

wearing a sign that said: "WILD STYLE TOURS: BEST PEOPLE WATCHING SINCE _____ . NO
                                                                           year you were born

BITING ALLOWED." Along for the ride there was a(n) _____ with a(n) _____ and _____ ,
                                                      animal   noun   noun

two _____ holding _____ , and a(n) _____ taking _____ .
     animal, plural   noun, plural   animal   noun, plural

Just then, they spotted me. "_____ !" one gasped. Then they all began to _____ and yell
                               exclamation   verb

"HUMAN!" Camera bulbs flashed left and right! The commotion grew louder as the group came closer.

21

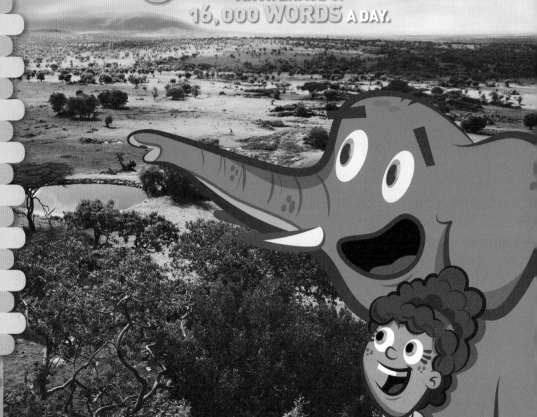

adjective

> verb ending in –ing

verb

> verb

verb

> noun

adjective

> something sweet

adjective

> adjective

adjective

> noun

past-tense verb

> past-tense verb

verb

> body part

direction

Fun Fact! HUMANS **SPEAK** AN AVERAGE OF **16,000 WORDS** A DAY.

Humans Can Talk?

"Calm down, everybody!" the tour guide yelled. "Remember the rules. One, humans are very _____ .
adjective
Absolutely no _____ . Two, if the human gets close to you, _____ immediately and
verb ending in –ing verb
_____ . Three, if the human growls at you, _____ and play _____ ." Then I heard
verb verb noun
a(n) _____ cheetah cub asks his mom if he could take me home as a pet. "No, _____ ,"
adjective something sweet
the mother replied. "You heard the guide. Humans are _____ ; they make _____ pets."
adjective adjective
A(n) _____ snake asked if she could feed me. They all seemed to talk as if I could not understand
adjective
them. Finally, I spoke up. "Can you help me? I'm looking for my _____ ," I explained. They all
noun
_____ and _____ . "I have never heard one talk before," a zebra said. They began asking
past-tense verb past-tense verb
me questions like how did I _____ on two legs and why did my _____ look like that.
verb body part
Finally, the elephant told me I should head _____ and ask the crocodiles if they had seen my group.
direction

- adjective
- number
- name of animal group
- adjective
- noun
- past-tense verb
- adverb ending in –ly
- noun
- adjective
- sound ending in –ing
- number
- adjective
- verb ending in –ed
- exclamation
- something gross
- animal
- favorite card game
- verb

Fun Fact! MALE LION CUBS STAY WITH THE PRIDE FOR **TWO YEARS** BEFORE MOM **CHASES** THEM OFF.

The trip to see the crocodiles was going to be a(n) _____ one—the river was _____ mile(s)
adjective _number_

away! Along the way, the lioness had to stop to tell her _____ where she was going. We
name of animal group

approached a(n) _____ _____ formation. As she crept closer, she _____ and told
adjective _noun_ _past-tense verb_

me to wait outside. She did not like the taste of humans, but her family might! I waited _____
adverb ending in –ly

by a(n) _____. Suddenly, I heard a(n) _____ _____ noise. "Who's there?" I
noun _adjective_ _sound ending in –ing_

shouted nervously. I turned around to see _____ _____ lion cub(s) spring out from behind a
number _adjective_

nearby bush. One charged right over and ... _____ me! " _____ !" he said.
verb ending in –ed _exclamation_

"You taste like _____ !" The cubs sniffed me for a while, then decided they did not want to eat
something gross

me. Instead, they invited me to play "Pin-the-Tail-on-the- _____ " and _____ . Our
animal _favorite card game_

games came to an abrupt end when the earth began to _____ under our feet. "What's that?" I asked.
verb

past-tense verb

past-tense verb

verb

noun

animal

noun

number

verb ending in –ed

adverb

adjective

past-tense verb

body part

adjective

direction

direction

noun

adjective

verb

Fun Fact! EACH YEAR, MORE THAN **ONE MILLION WILDEBEESTS** MIGRATE FROM **TANZANIA** TO **KENYA.**

Stampede!

"STAMPEDE!" the lion cubs shouted together. I didn't know what to do. I _____ (past-tense verb) left, then

I _____ (past-tense verb) right. Rocks were falling all around me. The lion cubs disappeared. I was about

to _____ (verb) up the rock when suddenly I was flung into the _____ (noun) and landed right on the

back of a(n) _____ (animal). I didn't know what to do. I was zooming as fast as a(n) _____ (noun) on top

of a(n) _____ (number) -pound animal! If I fell off, I would be _____ (verb ending in –ed), so I just held on

_____ (adverb)! The animal was clearly _____ (adjective). It bucked and _____ (past-tense verb),

trying to shake me. Finally, it threw me onto the _____ (body part) of another one! Then that one threw me,

too! They were clearly having a(n) _____ (adjective) time, tossing me _____ (direction) and _____ (direction)!

Then I saw my opportunity to escape. The _____ (noun) was ahead! If I could just wait until they were closer

I could dive into the _____ (adjective) river. Steady ... I thought. One ... two ... three ... _____ (verb)!

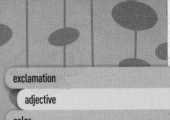

Word list

- exclamation
  - adjective
- color
  - past-tense verb
- adjective
  - body part
- adjective
  - color
- adjective
  - animal, plural
- U.S. state
  - adjective
- adjective
  - past-tense verb
- past-tense verb
  - adverb ending in –ly
- verb

Fun Fact! NILE CROCODILES CAN WEIGH OVER 1,600 POUNDS (725 KG)— AS MUCH AS FOUR LARGE AFRICAN LIONS!

Swimming With Crocs

With a(n) "_____ !" I landed in the _____ _____ water. I _____
exclamation   adjective   color   past-tense verb

on my back trying to figure out what to do. Sure, the crocodiles might know where my family is, but I wasn't

sure I wanted to get _____ enough to ask. Suddenly, out of the corner of my _____ ,
adjective   body part

I saw a(n) _____ _____ shadow drifting toward me ... then it disappeared. " _____
adjective   color   adjective

_____ of _____ !" I exclaimed. "What was that?" Then out of nowhere
animal, plural   U.S. state

a(n) _____ _____ snout rose above me. SPLASH! It crashed down in the water
adjective   adjective

as I _____ out of reach. Another figure rose up behind me. I was surrounded by crocodiles!
past-tense verb

I _____ as it tried to grab me. This must have scared the others, because they seemed to
past-tense verb

back off _____ . I had to get out of there! At that moment, a huge tail came up beneath
adverb ending in –ly

me. All it took was one big _____ and I was flying through the air!
verb

- adjective
  - adjective
- adjective
  - smelly food, plural
- body part, plural
  - silly name
- type of game
  - large number
- clothing item, plural
  - type of hat, plural
- verb
  - animal
- same animal
  - vegetable, plural
- vegetable, plural
  - favorite snack, plural
- favorite candy, plural
  - favorite dessert, plural
- liquid

30

Fun Fact!

A GROUP OF **HIPPOS** IS CALLED A **BLOAT.**

When I opened my eyes everything was _____ (adjective). It was _____ (adjective) and _____ (adjective) and smelled like rotten _____ (smelly food, plural). Suddenly, something grabbed me by my _____ (body part, plural). I was pulled out of the hole I was stuck in—and staring into the face of a hippo! "Sorry," he said. "You landed right in Uncle _____ (silly name)'s mouth. The kids are playing _____ (type of game) with his teeth, you see," the hippo said apologetically. "Welcome to our family reunion! Are you hungry?" he asked. I looked around and saw at least _____ (large number) hippos. Some were wearing _____ (clothing item, plural) and _____ (type of hat, plural) and playing games like "Hide-and-_____ (verb)" and "_____ (animal), _____ (same animal), Goose." Something smelled delicious. I looked around and saw a grill chock-full of _____ (vegetable, plural) and _____ (vegetable, plural). There was a table with bowls of _____ (favorite snack, plural), _____ (favorite candy, plural), and _____ (favorite dessert, plural). And to drink, there was _____ (liquid). "You're not going to eat me?" I asked. "Course not!" he said. "Hippos are vegetarians!"

adjective

large number

adjective

adjective

adjective

something gross

past-tense verb

your name

adjective

adjective

adjective

color

body part

silly noise

number

noun

adjective

Fun Fact! TO AVOID GETTING **SUNBURNED, RHINOS WALLOW** IN MUD.

Bird Brains

Just then I heard a(n) _____ rumbling noise. "Our friends have arrived!" the hippo announced.
adjective

_____ _____ rhinos came into view. They were _____ and _____
large number _adjective_ _adjective_ _adjective_

and smelled like _____ . I was afraid for a moment, but then one of them _____ at me.
something gross _past-tense verb_

"Forgive my manners," the hippo said. "I haven't even introduced you. What's your name?" "_____ ," I
your name

replied. "And I was wondering if you could help me." I told them my story. When I was finished, a(n) _____
adjective

_____ rhinoceros walked up to me. A(n) _____ _____ tickbird was sitting on his
adjective _adjective_ _color_

_____ . The rhino whispered something I could not hear. But the tickbird must have heard it because it
body part

suddenly flew up and called out a loud "_____ !" _____ other tickbird(s) flew up and joined
silly noise _number_

him. They came together in a huddle then broke apart and spelled out words in the sky! It read: "CALLING ALL

BIRDS. NEED HELP. LOST _____ . BE ON THE LOOKOUT FOR _____ VEHICLE."
noun _adjective_

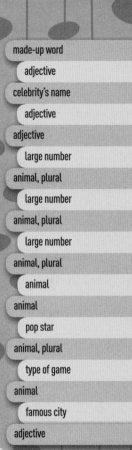

- made-up word
- adjective
- celebrity's name
- adjective
- adjective
- large number
- animal, plural
- large number
- animal, plural
- large number
- animal, plural
- animal
- animal
- pop star
- animal, plural
- type of game
- animal
- famous city
- adjective

Fun Fact! A **SPOTTED HYENA** CAN EAT EVERY PART OF ITS PREY—INCLUDING THE **BONES.**

African Traffic Jam

I doubted the birdcall would work, but I guessed it couldn't hurt. "Everybody ready to head out?" the hippo asked.

"Where?" I replied. "The safari party at _____ watering hole. It's going to be _____. They say
                                                    made-up word   adjective

_____ will be there. Climb aboard!" The hippo bent down for me to climb onto his _____
    celebrity's name   adjective

_____ back. I shrugged and pulled myself up. No sooner had we exited the brush than we were stopped dead in
    adjective

our tracks. "Traffic jam," the hippo explained. Sure enough, there were _____ _____ , _____
                                                                                                            large number   animal, plural   large number

_____ , and _____ _____ all patiently waiting at a standstill. A huge _____
 animal, plural   large number   animal, plural   animal

and a tiny _____ were groovin' to _____ on safari radio. Two _____ were playing a
                          animal   pop star   animal, plural

game of _____ . A(n) _____ was reading the _____ Times newspaper. "What's the
              type of game   animal   famous city

backup, bub?" the hippo asked a passing giraffe. The giraffe stretched out its _____ neck. "Looks like a
                                                                                                                            adjective

hyena collided with a gazelle. They're exchanging insurance information. We should start moving soon."

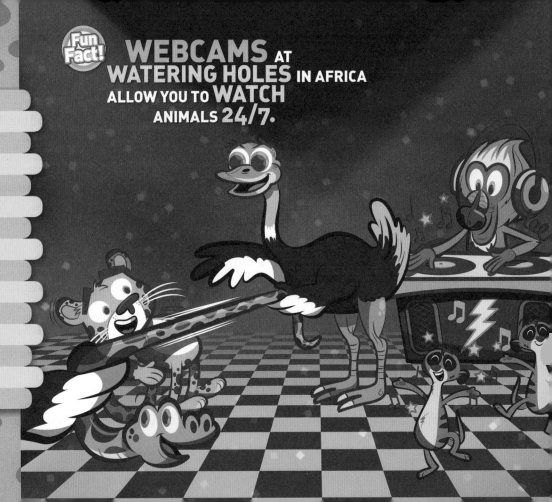

Fun Fact! WEBCAMS AT WATERING HOLES IN AFRICA ALLOW YOU TO WATCH ANIMALS 24/7.

- adjective
- adjective
- noun
- gymnastics move, plural
- type of music
- animal
- animal
- favorite song
- baby noise
- silly word
- silly word
- adjective
- insect, plural
- clothing item, plural
- type of dance

The safari party was in full swing when we finally arrived. It was like nothing I had ever seen! We squeezed past

two _____ water buffalo bouncers and made our way in. A(n) _____ gazelle wandered
        adjective   adjective

past with a(n) _____ on her head. There were cheetahs doing _____ into the pool.
              noun   gymnastics move, plural

A baboon deejay played _____ music, and a limbo line was forming behind two ostriches holding
                       type of music

a snake. There was a lineup of meerkats jumping off a(n) _____ , and a(n) _____ clown
                                                         animal   animal

making balloon humans. The party really got going when the deejay started playing " _____ "
                                                                                     favorite song

by Lady _____ and everyone rushed onto the dance floor. Elephants, giraffes, hippos, and rhinos
        baby noise

all joined in to do the _____ hop and the _____ twist. Everyone was getting into the
                        silly word   silly word

action! I looked down at my feet and saw two _____ _____ wearing
                                             adjective   insect, plural

_____ and dancing the _____ . This was some shindig!
clothing item, plural   type of dance

37

color

noun

time

noun

adjective

adjective ending in –ed

animal

noun

verb

noun

noun

noun, plural

animal, plural

adjective

animal

noun, plural

noun

Scary Skies

Suddenly everything grew dark. I looked up, and the sky was turning _____ . I checked my
_{color}

_____ , but it wasn't even close to _____ yet, and there wasn't a(n) _____
_{noun}   _{time}   _{noun}

in sight. Suddenly I realized thousands of _____ black shapes were filling the sky. The animals
_{adjective}

seemed _____ , too. I looked up at the _____ next to me, but he just
_{adjective ending in –ed}   _{animal}

stared at the _____ . Without warning, someone yelled, " _____ !" and all the animals
_{noun}   _{verb}

began to run for cover. The crocodiles dove in the _____ , and the ostriches buried their heads in
_{noun}

the _____ . The monkeys climbed up into the _____ , and the _____
_{noun}   _{noun, plural}   _{animal, plural}

began to stampede. I had to take cover, fast! I dove under a(n) _____ _____ ,
_{adjective}   _{animal}

but as it began to move, I decided maybe that wasn't the best idea. Finally, I spotted a table with

_____ and a(n) _____ sitting on it, and I crawled under it.
_{noun, plural}   _{noun}

Fun Fact!

A MAN MADE A VIDEO OF HIMSELF **FLYING** WITH HOMEMADE **BIRDS' WINGS**— BUT IT WAS A **FAKE!**

- past-tense verb
- large number
- species of bird
- species of bird
- species of bird
- noun, plural
- past-tense verb
- clothing item
- exclamation
- adjective
- verb ending in –ing
- exclamation
- noun
- body part, plural
- noun
- type of storm

The commotion outside began to die down. I _____ my head out to make sure the coast was clear and
_{past-tense verb}

realized what had been causing all the fuss. There were about _____ birds circling high in the air. "Looks
_{large number}

like your search party is back!" the hippo called to me. With that, a(n) _____ , a(n) _____ ,
_{species of bird} _{species of bird}

and a(n) _____ surrounded me. They flapped their _____ and _____ , but I
_{species of bird} _{noun, plural} _{past-tense verb}

couldn't understand them. Without warning, they grabbed me by my _____ and lifted me high into
_{clothing item}

the air. "_____ !" I yelled. "Put me down!" The _____ wind was so strong, I could barely
_{exclamation} _{adjective}

open my eyes. I finally managed to look down and saw all of my safari friends below me, _____ and
_{verb ending in –ing}

yelling, "_____ !" It was then I realized the birds must have found my safari group. "Thanks for
_{exclamation}

the _____ !" I called back. We continued to soar through the air until my _____
_{noun} _{body part, plural}

chattered and my _____ looked like I had been through a(n) _____ .
_{noun} _{type of storm}

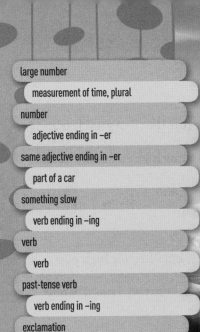

- large number
  - measurement of time, plural
- number
  - adjective ending in –er
- same adjective ending in –er
  - part of a car
- something slow
  - verb ending in –ing
- verb
  - verb
- past-tense verb
  - verb ending in –ing
- exclamation
  - animal sound
- adjective
  - adverb ending in –ly
- verb
  - verb

Fun Fact! WEIGHING UP TO 40 POUNDS (18 KG), AFRICA'S KORI BUSTARD MAY BE THE HEAVIEST FLYING ANIMAL.

Dropping In

After what seemed like _____ _____, we spotted the safari vehicle. It
             large number   measurement of time, plural

must have been going _____ mile(s) per hour! The birds flew _____ and
                        number   adjective ending in –er

_____—that's when I realized they were planning to lower me onto the _____!
same adjective ending in –er   part of a car

Right then I spotted a(n) _____ _____ on the road up ahead. The
                            something slow   verb ending in –ing

vehicle started to _____ and _____ to avoid the collision. Whew! It stopped just in time!
                      verb   verb

The birds _____ me onto the roof of the vehicle. It took a moment to get my balance, but
            past-tense verb

eventually I was _____. "_____!" I called as the birds flew away.
                  verb ending in –ing   exclamation

"_____!" they called back. Now how on earth was I going to get down? The answer was
   animal sound

obvious, but _____. I would have to jump onto the ground. _____, I began
                adjective   adverb ending in –ly

to _____ over to one side. I grabbed hold of the edge. One … two … three … _____!
     verb   verb

- body part
- nickname for mother
- nickname for father
- past-tense verb
- adjective
- large number
- something loud, plural
- adjective
- something large
- body part, plural
- large number
- adjective
- adjective
- adjective
- adjective
- adjective

Fun Fact! DURING ONE SLEEP STAGE, OUR **BODIES** BECOME **PARALYZED** SO WE DON'T ACT OUT OUR **DREAMS.**

44

The last thing I remember was seeing the ground come closer to my _____ as I fell
body part

to the earth. When I opened my eyes, my parents were standing over me. "_____ !
nickname for mother

_____ ! I found you!" I said. They looked at each other and _____ . "Found us?"
nickname for father   past-tense verb

Dad asked. "I didn't know we were missing!" I was _____ and confused. Dad's voice sounded
adjective

like _____ _____ and I felt like I had been hit by a(n) _____
large number   something loud, plural   adjective

_____ . "How many _____ am I holding up?" Mom asked. "_____ ," I
something large   body part, plural   large number

replied. "Where am I?" I asked. "At camp!" Mom said. "You've been here all day!" "No I haven't!" I said. "I've

been out on safari!" I told them about the _____ meerkat meal, the _____ stampede, the
adjective   adjective

_____ hippo reunion, and the _____ safari party. "Wow, what a day!" Mom laughed. "That
adjective   adjective

bump on your head must have been more _____ than we thought. You had quite a dream!"
adjective

adjective

   adjective

adjective

   noun ending in −ness

type of fruit

   animal, plural

animal, plural

   animal, plural

animal, plural

   type of vegetable

a profession

   animal, plural

food, plural

   past-tense verb

year you were born

   noun

Fun Fact! THE WORD "SAFARI" COMES FROM THE SWAHILI WORD FOR "JOURNEY."

The Proof Is in the Picture

It was *not* a dream! There's no way I could have imagined the _____ lioness, or the _____
adjective   adjective

tour group, or even the _____ crocodiles! My mom must have noticed the look of _____
adjective   noun ending in –ness

on my face, because she said, "Look, _____, here are the pictures from the safari your dad and I
type of fruit

went on today." I flipped through pictures of _____ and _____. There were even
animal, plural   animal, plural

_____ and _____. Could I be wrong? Maybe my safari adventure really hadn't
animal, plural   animal, plural

happened. "Don't worry, _____," my mom said. "The _____ said you'll be able to join us
type of vegetable   a profession

tomorrow." Man, they saw everything and I missed it, I thought. She even had a picture of two _____
animal, plural

eating _____. Just then, I noticed a tiny elephant wearing what looked like a sign in the background.
food, plural

I _____ in as much as I could. And there, in teeny tiny letters, I read: "WILD STYLE TOURS: BEST
past-tense verb

PEOPLE WATCHING SINCE _____". I smiled to myself and drifted off to _____.
year you were born   noun

Credits

Cover, Perseo Medusa/Shutterstock; 4, AnnaIA/Shutterstock; 6, My Good Images/Shutterstock; 8, Galyna Andrushko/Shutterstock; 10, Tupungato/Shutterstock; 12, Chantal de Bruijne/Shutterstock; 14, Graeme Shannon/Shutterstock; 16, Jason Finlay/Shutterstock; 18, Jakub Gruchot/Shutterstock; 20, PHOTOCREO Michal Bednarek/Shutterstock; 22, PHOTOCREO Michal Bednarek/Shutterstock; 24, Totajla/Shutterstock; 26, Stacey Ann Alberts/Shutterstock; 28, Peter Gudella/Shutterstock; 30, Karl W./Shutterstock; 32, Pal Teravagimov/Shutterstock; 34, Isabella Pfenninger/Shutterstock; 36, Lightspring/Shutterstock; 38, Eric Isselée/Shutterstock; 40, Pakhnyushcha/Shutterstock; 42, Oleg Znamenskiy/Shutterstock; 44, Konstantin L./Shutterstock; 46, Dolores Giraldez Alonso/Shutterstock

---

Published by the National Geographic Society

Gary E. Knell, *President and Chief Executive Officer*
John M. Fahey, *Chairman of the Board*
Declan Moore, *Executive Vice President; President, Publishing and Travel*
Melina Gerosa Bellows, *Publisher; Chief Creative Officer, Books, Kids, and Family*

Prepared by the Book Division

Hector Sierra, *Senior Vice President and General Manager*
Nancy Laties Feresten, *Senior Vice President, Kids Publishing and Media*
Jennifer Emmett, *Vice President, Editorial Director, Kids Books*
Eva Absher-Schantz, *Design Director, Kids Publishing and Media*
Jay Sumner, *Director of Photography, Kids Publishing*
R. Gary Colbert, *Production Director*
Jennifer A. Thornton, *Director of Managing Editorial*

Staff for This Book

Shelby Alinsky, *Project Editor*
James Hiscott, Jr., *Art Director*
Kelley Miller, *Senior Photo Editor*
Becky Baines, *Writer*
Jason Tharp, *Illustrator*
Ariane Szu-Tu, *Editorial Assistant*
Callie Broaddus, *Design Production Assistant*
Margaret Leist, *Photo Assistant*
Grace Hill, *Associate Managing Editor*
Joan Gossett, *Production Editor*
Lewis R. Bassford, *Production Manager*
Susan Borke, *Legal and Business Affairs*

Production Services

Phillip L. Schlosser, *Senior Vice President*
Chris Brown, *Vice President, NG Book Manufacturing*
Rachel Faulise, *Manager*
Rahsaan Jackson, *Imaging*

Editorial, Design, and Production by Plan B Book Packagers

The National Geographic Society is one of the world's largest nonprofit scientific and educational organizations. Founded in 1888 to "increase and diffuse geographic knowledge," the Society's mission is to inspire people to care about the planet. It reaches more than 400 million people worldwide each month through its official journal, *National Geographic*, and other magazines; National Geographic Channel; television documentaries; music; radio; films; books; DVDs; maps; exhibitions; live events; school publishing programs; interactive media; and merchandise. National Geographic has funded more than 10,000 scientific research, conservation, and exploration projects and supports an education program promoting geographic literacy.

For more information, please call 1-800-NGS LINE (647-5463) or write to the following address:

National Geographic Society, 1145 17th Street N.W.
Washington, D.C. 20036-4688 U.S.A.

Visit us online at nationalgeographic.com/books

For librarians and teachers: ngchildrensbooks.org

More for kids from National Geographic: kids.nationalgeographic.com

For information about special discounts for bulk purchases, please contact National Geographic Books Special Sales: ngspecsales@ngs.org

For rights or permissions inquiries, please contact National Geographic Books Subsidiary Rights: ngbookrights@ngs.org

ISBN: 978-1-4263-1708-8

Printed in Hong Kong

14/THK/1